200mlf
4/86

# LIAR'S DICE

# LIAR'S DICE
# CAROL FROST

## ITHACA HOUSE
### ITHACA

Grateful acknowledgement is made to the editors of the following magazines for permission to reprint many of these poems: *Agni Review, Antaeus, Back Door, Beloit Poetry Journal, Chariton Review, Chowder Review, Cutbank, Falcon, Mississippi Review, New River Review, Occurence, Poetry Miscellany, Poetry Northwest, Prairie Schooner, Southern Poetry Review, Virginia Quarterly Review*. Also to Greywolf Press for permission to reprint poems from the chapbook *The Salt Lesson*. "Getting It Right" is reprinted from *The Massachusetts Review*, copyright 1978, The Massachusetts Review, Inc.

"Water Sounds": copyright 1976 by The Antioch Review, Inc. First published in *The Antioch Review*, Vol. 35, No. 3. Reprinted by permission of the editors.

Also "Memories" and "A Bed on the Floor": copyright 1978.

ITHACA HOUSE
108 N. Plain St.
Ithaca, New York   14850
Ithaca House books are distributed by SBD,   1636 Ocean View Ave., Kensington, CA   94707

Library of Congress Cataloging in Publication Data
Frost, Carol. 1948-
      Liar's Dice.

      I. Title.
PS3556.R596L5      811'.5'4      78-16125
ISBN 0-87886-098-3

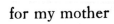

for my mother

# CONTENTS

## PARTIAL LIGHT

# THE BABY VARIATIONS

## DICE

# PARTIAL LIGHT

# THE WEATHER HORSE

The neighbor's horse has grown white this winter.
Imperfect in December,
now the horse is white as an avalanche.
I hear him under his fur:
and under the polar cap on the farmland there is
                                        wheezing.
His lungs are red with wind.
The ground is covered with fall's kill,
where green will concentrate.
Where worms discriminately chew
and mediaeval bugs in air holes breathe,
nitrogen and water go deep to fill the leg-sized roots.
The horse hasn't heard any of this, is too beautiful to
                                        care.

When his horse-hair falls out
and nudges the snow to melt,
he thunders from the trough to the shed,
he smells his own lather the more,
he whips the flies from his back with an insouciant
                                        tail.

He searches for a spouse.
When he marries her the sun stands still,
the sun having ever to shine on the horse's back.

## ALL SUMMER LONG

The dogs eat hoof slivers and lie under the porch.
A strand of human hair hangs strangely from a fruit
                                        tree
like a cry in the throat.  The sky is clay for the child
                                  who is past
being tired, who wanders in waist-deep
grasses.  Gnats rise in a vapor,
in a long mounting whine around her forehead and
                                        ears.
The sun is an indistinct moon.  Frail sticks
of grass poke her ankles
and a wet froth of spiders touches her legs
like wet fingers.  The musk and smell
of air is as hot as the savory
terrible exhales from a tired horse.

The parents are sleeping all afternoon
and no one explains the long uneasy afternoons.
She hears their combined breathing and swallowing
salivas, and sees their sides rising and falling
like the sides of horses in the hot pasture.

At evening a breeze dries and crumbles
the sky, and the clouds float like undershirts
and cotton dresses on a clothes line.  Horses
rock to their feet and race or graze.
Parents open their shutters and call
the lonely, happy child home.
The child who hates silences talks and talks
of cicadas and the manes of horses.

# THE SALT LESSON

Looking inside the bony plate, perceive
the gray sponge matter that from its depth
breeds without moving.
Colors belong to the surface, reckon
with the wind mounting tidal waves,
clouds' cover, or a ripple of sun.

Underneath, the seeping calculation,
the dark crevasses and only spots of artificial
light. What the mind allows, sucks
without bloat. Unearthly life,
a grouper eats a man whole, the gold
doubloons; something precious,

spontaneous. The gull returns to the sea
food broken down by sharks.
The mind is a sullen scavenger
with the belly and bowels of a god.

Water city, this impure taker
returns so little, a bubble of stupidity,
a salt piece of itself, of what it endures.

## THE BLUE CHAIR

At four in the morning
the radioactive hands
of the clock look less official.
It doesn't matter if it is 10 a.m. in Europe.
In some provinces it is a Catholic holiday. It is a fine
                                                    morning.
The small arms of the clock remind more of a
                                    child's chair
(not the real thing), miniature in the early hours.
I decide to go fishing. I follow the fish

to points of land where the sun heats
the water to 55 degrees.
I have brought the small chair
with my package lunch taped under the seat
to rest near when the morning slows.
It is a beautiful enamel blue rocker
which I watch as if I were watching
the lip of the milk in a jar
to keep me from spilling it if I walk.

The stream is too fast. There are no points.
There is no cover for the fish.
I eat the sandwiches. I tie rocks to the chair
and drop it into the water. Right away fish
                                    congregate
in the eddy of the blue rocker.
After a rest they begin to feed.
Trout eat minnows.
Suckers pull in pieces of plants sluicing by.
I wade to the chair
and catch fish with my hands.

It is like a factory.
In five hours I have finished the stream.

The water is devoid of fish
and on the bank is a struggling cloud of them.
I lift out the chair and the river is fast again.
It is no longer early.
I leave the slow fish in the sun
for the birds.  I take two prize
fish home.  I have no more use for the chair.

## FAMILY

                    The sprawling vegetable
venders, lettuce blown like leaves
I couldn't recognize, the monastery roof
going to seed, excess of tabled fish in this climate;
spitting, blind ends, vendors and bargains;
this loose Mediterranean acre.
The sun baking off the market's indifference.

A woman's dark tattoos: ant hills,
fluted grass. An orchard of messages.
Bruised fruit, the walnut-colored hoe
blade grown into the hungry bark;
grafting, droughts, the seed in the palm
of the hand. The single jewel
that is a touch of water or glass on the forehead:
light in a tree.

There are children balky as calves,
stiff-legged and damp. Fourteen calves
and five uncles. They walk as slow as I
and regard me—the children, the uncles.
To the end of the street. The herd curious
and brilliant.
They stop at the boundary
and protect each other.

# A WOMAN WITH HER PLANTS TALKING

People keep giving me plants.
I must be loved, surreal.  Succulants.
I stole asparagus fern from my tenant,
potted it for my green bedroom.
The mother plant molded and coated the bulbs
like tongues in the dirt.  The tenant has handsome
                                                legs.

I water the little green animals
who push up their bare heads gratefully
then talk in long vowels in the wet air.

The men with white veins for feet.
Plants with beards and double chins.
Today for a lamp, I have more friends.
The humid soil, their dirt up my fingernails,
the lovely card table by the window that eats sun
for them and smiles.  The striped tiger upstairs.
What polished ivy creeps
on my arm—a badgered pet?
The male tiger in the rafters.
The fern sticks on my pillow, moss pillow,
and winds its vegetable feet nearer,
knowing it is not a caterpillar.
If the bed would just make itself fold
to swallow me.  To die in secretions.
I buck in that satin shell,
try to break the jungle.  Come, orange tiger.
By day I shine all their leaves,
see my face hundreds of times as if in dark paintings.

## ICE STORM

A complex budding twig, like a trilobite
encased in cold amber forever,
is frozen this morning in a clear cast
its own shape.  And trees are bent
by unearthly ice.  Sleet flies through
the old sky to cover parks and roads.
A shining swarm.  Ice locusts.

Ice lights a pail.  Yesterday's mud
is chitinous with it.  Still, the magic
takes place.  Presto.  A barn becomes a statue.
A swing set brightens.  Whatever movement
is too slight to see:  I think
of molecules faintly zooming under the crust.
The light is astonishing.

The ice will melt, says a voice
from the radio.  Then the leaves will wriggle
in the air for two seasons.  I am
in my car following another.  I shut off
the radio.  To have this perfect ice!
The cars shine like mica.  A layer
of ice, diaphanous, rockets

up from the roof of the preceding car.
I lean to the window to measure the trajectory.
The ice is luminous.  This is dangerous
to be so fascinated.  Coo-coo, signals an oncoming
driver with a finger to his head.  I should

sit in a dream chair? The glass rocket
flies apart in mid-air. The cars are peeled.

The end of the storm is ambiguous.
Stalagmite grass in the filleted light
keeps for hours hundreds of designs.
A rock or cigarette pack in the ice ditch
looks like a remarkable fossil. Repairmen
fasten on the trees and poles like insects,
while statues darken and the day melts.

## THIS NORTH

Hardy green cress
under ice water, I'd ache to touch.  Green
as a boy's voice in all the snow
a valley can hold, calling go
to the spotted cows.
Their dung a small mountain.
The sun steaming:  light smoke coming from the
                                                west.

Dusk from the east.
Central, a piece of hide foreign
to the snow,
a femur outcrop to step across, a buried voice
the wind raises, heart.  Heat to my chin;
a thrill of ice central.

## CORAL

What's left of the sea pulse above water
is murderous spires.
The animal is no longer soft and giving.
Spires to the sun.
                That glint in someone's eye
that is piece by piece
too comfortless.

She walks to the flashing sea,
the skeletal, wedged caves of coral
and jumps clear.
There sunken colors, blessed sand
to lie on without the burden
of air.

        In calendars of rain
until a sounding she cannot resist in her ears and
                       temples.

And fish like small bells.
Fish like small bells.

## POTATO EATERS

### after Van Gogh

They do not emerge
from the clumsy room
until new light is brought
and they savor morning potatoes.
The sun scours their limbs,
the sparse walls and furniture.

Naive, they wander outdoors.
The bits of potato on the platter
are all that's left of their homely
altar. They go to their work,
superb. To bring them to their senses
we work them to exhaustion

of certain light, uncertain madness.
They feel us breathing
on their backs and hold their collars
as if cold. We are barely aware
of what fright we cause in them.
They offer us potatoes.

## LIKE HIS MOTHER

In the morning
when all the lights in the house are on,
I know you have been afraid
of what comes to you night after night,
the dream of yourself,
the child at the top of the darkened stairway
calling in a stranger's voice.

You turned on the hallway light,
but shadows sang from the railing and yourself.
Huddled, you saw over your shoulder
a darker boy kneel by the rough wall.
You were like

his mother and went into the dark
room and lit it
with a stroke of your hand.  Over and over,
all the rooms, until there was no more fear.
In your room this morning you might sleep naked,
where you held the other boy to you
to make him warm.

As if you were his mother, you leaned your head to
                                              his

and whispered
a story about twilight
your mother whispered to you
and, almost absently, made the darkness yours.

## THE BLACK AND WHITE
## PHOTOGRAPHER

The woman looks to the light
in a picture that does her more than justice.
She misses the gay parasols,
lace stencils on the walls which appear as smoke,
her print dress. She maintains black
is not flattering. She looks to the light
which softens a lacquered cabinet,
which dissolves half her eye,
which makes one hand seem like a fist
and one a reclining nude.
I have fallen in love with this woman
and her damask pride.
I take her portrait again and again.

## KING MIDAS

At the exact instant of magic
the circumstance of a gold coin
falling on a wood table told me
to choose that wish: I turned
a jeweled bird into gold

and could have gold forever . . .
It made me sullen
after trays and trays of fruit
were brought to me so I could eat
and I couldn't eat

since my lips were as potent
as my fingers. I couldn't feel
my wife. My servants hid,
and the moment I wished I hadn't wished
for everything I fell ill

onto deliriously yellow sheets.
Since it was too good and too determined
a dream, I came to—hating replicas.
There was subtle light altered
by the glass bird

on the coverlet. Something vague.
And I fell in love with crystal
and the light. I keep a hard nugget
of gold under my tongue to remind
me of the worst thirst.

Mornings I walk through my moors
to the cold lake.  It is so early, larks
still sing to themselves.  The ice rim
and the whole dark center of the water
are lit by the honest sun.

## THE UNDRESSING

They took off their clothes 1000 nights
and felt the plaster of the moon
sift over them, and the ground roll
them in its dream. Little did they know
the light and clay and their own sweat
became a skin they couldn't wash away.
Each night bonded to the next,
and they grew stiffer.  They noticed this
in sunlight—there were calluses,
round tough moons on their extremities,
shadows under their eyes,
and sometimes a faint sour smell
they hadn't had as children.
It worried them, but at night the animal
in their bodies overcame their reluctance
to be naked with each other,
and the mineral moon did its work.
At last when they woke up and were dead,
statues on their backs in the park,
they opened their mouths
and crawled out, pitifully soft and small,
not yet souls.

## THE OLIVE JUG

Every spare detail. If you replace the olives
in an unearthed jug, use ones
that are as black.
A new olive
would be a dead giveaway.

Stealing a Schwinn bike outside the museum
to kidnap a political foe,
alter it barely. The thinning edge of a coin,
the yellow nose of the market brass boar.
Don't change the sex.

To take a lover
be open to a frill in his voice.
Ride side saddle if you have to,
but listen to every particle
of speech.  The bare bones are not enough.

Take the fingerprints to your heart.
Cornered in hot lights,
rub your own leg, blame finding the jug.
Deny, deny.

# ELEUTHERA

### 1.

The general sunlight moves like wind across
the coral with its fine undulating whips
and coral where white chickens peck for seeds.
We wake to small sounds:
a reign of tapping on the coast.
And if we look, leaves and leaves of silver
float on the once plain sea.
We rise from the mosaic of dream
and step across a gritty floor.

### 2.

At the corner of the porch a lizard clings
like a statue to its pedestal.
There is no reason to frighten
the old creature. If we look closely
in its seed-sized eyes, is fear in
the seed-sized figures? In a flicker,
as a single dead leaf might turn over
to a breeze, the lizard is gone.

### 3.

On the other side of the island the entrails
of the chickens are fed to a thousand sharks.
The bloody, roiling pit. The stray bite.
Those who come to watch
and stand flat against the sky are hypnotized,
seem to hold their breath for minutes
and expel it—like a taut line snapping,
a sharp laugh, or sorrow.
Tonight their sleep is different.

4.

Everywhere the smell of chickens.
As we travel the Queen's Highway,
broken silos are the remains
of another culture.  A pregnant
woman tells us they held water.

At the Glass Window the island is level
with the ocean, mid-day underwater.
White patches of gentle sand and blackened coral
map the solemn inequalities of the world.

5.

We are cut at the waist and crown
the clear shallows.  Our legs elongate.
Our torsos are bronze and jeweled by water drops.
The sea air has begun to stretch our lungs
and later when they ache we'll catch
one hand to our chests and be glad.

We return to our darkened vacation rooms
and play a wax recording of Paganini.
It is as if a star began to streak.
And the invisible wind pushes the sea up and up
the cement steps of the dock
in rhythms the night coming on
provokes us to hear.  We enter the cage of sleep.

## KILLING THE DOG

The dog you shot has littered the yard
with jawbones and gnawed hooves
of slaughtered yearlings.

                You learn this
a summer later, mowing the terraces of weeds
north of the house.  A pig's tooth in your pocket

at first, soon the cotton cloth by your hip
is bulging.  The mower is full of gas.
The blade spins and the sound, like birds

escaping, of it scattering grey bone scares you.
Yon lean on the mower.  It whirrs and roars.
You have to turn your head.

               The north
side of the farm has no windows.  No one has seen
you flinch.  But you turn off the mower.

You walk to the house and sit with your back
pressed full on the wall.  It's hot and still:
as if the house held you.  The mower cools.

The pieces of bone in your pocket dig
in your groin.

              The dog was a nuisance.
Smelled.  Submit, submit, it growled
in the tulips.  Chased horses and riders.

You flush in the heat.  You empty your pocket.
The chips are discolored, more
like shattered porcelain than bone.

The sun that whitens this field.
As if under snow or the sky turned over,

you are afraid.  The birds fly upside down.
You count through strata.
You call on and dread a neighbor.

## APPALOOSA, DEAD CAT

Appaloosa, dead cat in October merge with the
                                    sodden ground.
Horse is partly mist,
and cat's blood with hanks
of grey fur slickens the weed.  What translucent
                                    cloaks
touch land and animal!  What poised light
on the grimace of the sallow tomcat!
Dank branch, smudged horse pelt—will nothing
                                    stir?

Only seep?
I in the womb-warm field want a cold cadenza
of sun;  startle the hills and birdsong,
Appaloosa, dead cat stir red
in a last light.

## BONFIRE MAKERS

Sharks' teeth light.  The sand bald,
first, as if it were far away.
Closer, its cellars and mountains of glass,
its jaws; the bonfire catches
and the sand cannot stand still.

A shadow leaps to a growing dune
like a sword eel through weeds.  Where
does it go?
                    The fire clicks its tongue and teeth.
Scarf, face, star in the sand.  Our faces
snagged on a shining bone of light.

Our icy eyes.  The picket fence
in our faces.  Hold a red hand up—
shipwreck, tangle of veins.

The wind blows the other way
and we are bodiless; fish skin
and navies of shadows.  Too dark,
too dark.  We call for spawn,
prey, clear water ribs, and
faces and fins of light in the salt lagoons.

# THE PARADISE ZOO

The sun mixes with the dust and excrement
of this animal pavement and jams the air.
The central fountain is broken.
Moisture corrodes the lip of the ornamental pool
and the sweaty pennies thrown by children.
                                    Freshened
by a small breeze off the surface of the brackish water,
a soaking towel, people take their children's hands
and, having seen the tumble-down lions, march to
                        the monkey arcade.

Pure, high-pitched, careless chatter.
Mussed fur. Garbage eaters. They are not soured
or hurt by our nit-picking, fascinated attention.
They ball up their bodies
and hurl themselves, criss-cross, to the ceiling of
                        their domain,
balance and dance obscenely, plummet to a swing
near to earth like bedlamites, mug,
devour feces and frighten children
by extending parrot hands beyond the iron
bars, the iron-tasting air.
                        Shush the children
with an idea of cotton candy, and ignore
awhile longer the stink a jungle would absorb,
and think of their stolen jungle:
the shapes of sunlight in the woven, woven air,
water beads like chosen shells
on surfaces, tree reverting to earth,
earth earth, an old earth. Horizons concealed and
                        unnecessary.

Animals feeding or placid,
the smell of iron their own blood;

blood of their own moods.
Making sounds and hearing answers;
less emparadised than free.

## SOVEREIGN BEAR

There is a bear before us
we saw caged, lumberous;
ears fly-sore, coat darkened by the loss
of year long snows

and by a residue of steel
when he resisted the wall.
Rocking to and fro, turtle-
necked, immovable

as a bolted-down toy,
he seemed momentarily
domesticated, until with a scary
suddenness he turned his lord's eye

on us and stood up pawing
the air, as though he could dig
himself through air out of our king-
dom, stretched big

as we might come to know
in his gross land of snow
and blood-hunger. Soul-
less, sovereign and so

cunning; his mammal beauty
makes us shudder. After his prey
has tried to flee
and felt the stinging, instinctual joy

of his claw swing,
this grim genius of killing
eats, perfected, to kill again.
For us there is nothing

everyday as vigilant or cruel.
We stand near his childish hemisphere, all
changelings admiring the final
brutishness behind the thin wall.

What legendary ice or extinction
now?  The bear pads to his alien
hut and lolls on the ground
like an old tom, and we return

to the city, degrees warmer
in its center's misting glare.
If we can see it, what star
will point us to the mad perimeter,

the rime, where the beast learns
to walk almost like a man?

# FAT CHILDREN

Colossal boys and girls who go steady
with each other at the pool swim like walruses.
The water heaves them and is heaved when they
    belly

flop in suits and bathing dresses. Their limbs float
and shiver white as snow. The innocence with which

they move a strap, a hip, an eye, and look at goose
    bumps.
All the hope that's rolled-up under their stomachs
for deep love.  They're cold to their fathers and
    mothers

who are their parents and warn them to believe
    them.
And fear shark appetites, the trembling

kiss, blood ebbing through an eyelid.  Don't glance
at strangers.  They watch the heavy water and in
    unison
dive to nine feet in their dreams and hold hands.

## THE RITUAL OF THE URN

The women with their pink
plastic spoons are in the dayroom.
There is a large ornamental
coffee urn on the table
which is aluminum and rectangular.
Ten women sitting in conference
fashion at six-thirty a.m.  One
slaps down a hand
on the table and says, "I won't
be back," and nods.  The women
nod.  The room
is also a rectangle, and the women
are on the large ornamental
coffee urn facing like pears
their own faces, but staring
at the coffee spoons.  Shuffles
under the table.  A new nurse
enters and sees twenty-one
pairs of eyes as she circles
the coffee urn and taps 20
shoulders.  She says, "Good morning,
time to wash the floors."
Linoleum.  The living
rectangle stands.  Ten women file
out and ten women walk further
and further
into the shining coffee urn.

# A BED ON THE FLOOR

The wind beats dry thunder all night,
a sound of blankets snapping on a clothes line,
a sheet of tin roof we found as children
and shook in an untended field
ringed with project houses,
crows and bees flying their dark way,
rattles from the fury of bees and glass jars,
dogs and horses,
our running away from a prank.
Some fathers knocked terror into us.
Our bad laughter.

I lie down on the floor—
as I used to lie and hear
under my fierce child's grief
a motor hum, a furnace in the earth,
or someone crooning,
not forlornly, as if from a cellar,
a song in a dark idiom
about tribulation and mercy.
As a child will, I slept
with whatever sadness
on the humming floor.

## GETTING IT RIGHT

An arthritic she-goat cannot settle
to the packed earth unless hands sway
her bag of milk out of her knees' way.
This woman has never touched
a goat, the distended pouch so much like a child's
     belly,
but the dignified getting half-way down and
     inevitably up,
like a failure to depart,
or an image of the slack carcass hung like the wet coat
of a person in a hurry
overcomes her finickiness about the stench
of strong milk and goats' meat.
She straddles the goat,
lifts her as the sun rolls overhead,
and tries to get it right.

## NIGHT IS NO MORE OR LESS IMPORTANT THAN BAD CIRCLES OR 'KSING'

for Richard Hugo

Sick stomach. Bix Beiderbeck
rolling and keeping his horn like a small boat
on the swell of jazz. I'm trying to read poetry
to fall asleep. Flies
dropping like pelicans in the bed.
I brush them, sick, away
who live in the windows and lose them at night.
They fly bad circles.

My husband's sock, a drooping pet
with its otter smell, clings
though I have thrown it off the bed.
My son starts a song with remarkable swing
about cereal and birds — the feeder we hung.
He chortled at eating a bird's wing at lunch.
Everything is equal for food
and poetry. "Ksing," closing down
of the cymbal. High hat.

Who would eat flies? Words?
Bits of used wax paper, wings or fish scales on the
    bed,
small black ovals, their heads little gritty orchids,
these flies broken up in the storm and noise
of my thrashing to sleep. Bird hieroglyphics
and a fuzz of parts float like cream in the air.
The rhythm of song and horn rocking the night
takes me around, "ksing," around
in the whirlpool of recognized things.

## SPRING

**1.**

The tin ceiling is an authentic backdrop.
A donut hangs from a string.
Its pirouetting invites a touch,
but the putty-colored skin looks dusty
with mites.  There is a sign behind the bar
that offers prizes to the "bird-eater."
I have a drink and the bartender tells me
I won't want the donut anymore.
It has hung like an egg-tree
for five years.  A breeze of the insects
swirls on my arm.  I am a new carrier.

**2.**

Back in the striking sun,
I see through my eyelids.
I am off-guard.  A man's shadow
blends into mine, making it darker.
We stand together like gulls beside a skiff,
staring out on the white flats.
The sea breathes on us,
until focusing shows the dry cement.
What was that salt in the wind?
The man walks on.

**3.**

Rag-picking, I can't loosen the scarves
and towels I've bound on my arms
and torso.  I feel every inch
of my skin, the blood rising and

pounding like heat in radiator pipes.
A swarm of bees attracted to my sweat
must fly off the padding. You,
husband, and the children must feed me,
smooth me onto cool bedding.
Open a window. I will be fine in a day.

4.
At night I wake myself.
In the clear air I see a lamp,
a small book. My husband
is on his side. I close my eyes.
I hear rain. There are mice
in the walls. I think the room,
the darkness are mine.
My arms feel good on the bed.
There is a sigh. I connect
no meaning from object
to object to object.

# THE BABY VARIATIONS

after the painting by Gustav Klimt (1862-1918)

## BABY
### after Gustav Klimt

The nascent, slatted eyes
and patient face, the high
tinged copy of a bland world.

A dumb hymn, a naked
head, unhaunted, unabashed.
White beach, whiter moon.

The small-featured,
strange and sexless
giant we surround with bawdy

night gown and day gown.
Embroideries,
thread, purple bodice,

coral, deep voice
of the sky and sea
to come.  Shank

cloth, the maw of a storm,
musky flowers.  Please grow
and be checked

by all that we give you,
this sea of a dress.
Be civil and haunted.

## KLIMT'S BABY

In a salt marsh
among a texture of weeds
a baby lies.
A woman has just left.
The sea changes color
all day.  Nobody speaks
or comes.  The baby listens
to its own cries.  Eels
are hidden in the evening
shallows.
We know there is danger
in the black barge of
clouds that comes this way,
but we must wait, we think,
for the women to come back.
We concentrate
on the pure, patient
face of the child.
And we tell ourselves
the sea is a quilt,
the quilt the baby wears
is a calm sea,
the baby will live.

## THE QUILT

In the painting the baby wears all the clothes
she will ever wear; and every grimy dawn,
every fragment of afternoon, every
blood kiss is spun for her.  Riches, too.
Terrestrial,

of her silken name,
and the silver leaf of a tribal moon.
A thick quilt that clings like a water
fall.  Her rainbow, her soft, black secrets.
And, soon, as she grows, her arching body.

As she grows the quilt is used up
in her hands as she rubs and rubs
the cotton nap, and her fingers ache and
strengthen,
and she does and gives all that was

a long time ago beyond her.
What is left is a cloth medallion,
a cotton penny,
a minute before she knows she will die.
In the next painting perfect white.

# RHYME

Baby, baby, tiny doll
catch a finger, and don't fall.
If you holler, let you go,
baby, baby, tiny doll.

Baby, baby, little man
catch a papa, yes you can.
He won't like it when you're grown,
baby, baby, little man.

Baby, baby, tiny girl
catch a finger, and don't fall.
If you holler, let you go,
baby, baby, tiny girl.

Baby, baby, tiny doll
catch a finger, and hold on.
When you're grown up, I'll be gone.
Holler, holler, tiny doll.

## THE SONG OF THE NEWBORN

Sometimes I am afraid. The sounds of giants
wake me. No more the silent arrangement
of pools and birdcalls.
Giants thrash in the underbrush and fall
over the harmless roots,
sometimes beat
each other. Their blood hurts my eyes.

They say I have nothing in my eyes.
I have enough.

## THE HAND

The world was a foggy beach to those bright eyes,
haunted by rocks that were not there
until they were all that was there,

and shapes or shades that flew in the white wind.
As if a sheet had been loosely tied on the head.
It was no use looking very far.

And yet the beach was warm.  The ocean rose
and fell, rocking something large, or so it sounded,
and a white and blue-veined bird

sometimes hovered in the air right by.
Veins like rivers and white sand, white snow.
A bird that seemed like the whole world.

## THE FACTORY

Rayon is made here.
Dyes are made here
in vats. Tree-green, harlequin
yellow and purple.
You have never seen a sky of this hue.

We take the rayon and sell it,
machine to your clownish hands.
There are no flaws.
There are no flaws.
Make a dress for your daughter.

She'll wear a rainbow.
We make the rainbows,
solid boulevards of color.
Conch pink, mermaid blue.
Nature has less variety.

## THE DRESS

The sheer sheath dress is dry
and ancient and disheveled as a beached shark;
milder than a shark when worn by ordinary women
and live on hips in bright music.
Abused and slightly torn by the sea,
laced with salt, the dress takes dominion
over the other worldly debris—
rope, bottles, bows and scum.
Was it accidental?  Did a woman fall
from a great ship or a rented skiff?
How long did her perfume last in the air
above her plunge?  She sink faster than her dress?
Or under a brilliant, carnal sky
did she fold down her alluring dress to the deck,
kick it with the side of her foot so it slid
into the slow waves, and nod her mortal, innocent
                                                            head?

## TEAR

Let the baby be semi-
conscious of the change
today in the April air.
Her pastel cheek is warm
as blossoms in a cranny.

Grandfather is cold as stone
the sun forsakes.  Lamb
days past, the fickle sharp wind
strikes.  Let the baby be.
Babe cries and a blossom drops.

# DICE

## ADVICE TO AN INFATUEE

Keep as even tempered as possible.
Get his cat's name.
If he has no cat, learn what brand of beer he drinks.
    Bicycle by his house nonchalantly.
    Take a cast of his footprints.
    Walk through his dust on a sunny day.
    Hand him smaller and smaller objects
    until his fingers touch your hand.
Rummage through his wastebaskets for clues
to his habits.  Copy one habit.
After he rises from a chair sidle over to it
and sit where it's warm.
    Don't leave more buttons unbuttoned.
    Don't scowl along your nose.
    Don't let on.
Be open and closed at the same time:
be like a Chinese proverb or a beaded door.
If he looks at you meaningfully, become
a piece of sculpture with remarkable green/
gray/brown/hazel eyes,
    and think, "We have come this far,"
    or, "We must change our lives."
    Smile like a universe and a hurt child.
    Rehearse.  Wear sublime underwear.

## MIMICRIES

We have taken them into our houses:
orphans who danced the rhumba, Caribbean
waters, glances
from strangers, smoke that consumed
a waterfall, sea cucumbers, mantises
and the odor of semen.

               Not only for the love
of strangeness
have we collected this bric-a-brac—
the exquisite absence of touch
when a woman's forehead doesn't quite lean
on her lover's belt
becomes their remoteness when one of them goes
                     away.

Unlike our children who populate bark
boats with whole lineages
and send them innocently to sink
in the stormy drainage ditch,
we know what we do, collecting
images of frailty and passion.

If a songbird is raised without
hearing the song of his species
he will develop incomprehensible
vocal sounds never heard in nature.
*The New York Times*

## ABNORMAL SONG

Tired of our own voices asking
always the same question, sing-song,
the same preen in small talk,
bright feathers of the dialect

of longing, we learn less from birds
than we might have wished.
Gone to listen in a scrubbed field
in simplifying winter how less cold

a white-crown sings the day,
we don't hear normal song.
He's heard another melody
in tanner shrubs, his fellows singing

lower notes here over the hill.
He's never heard his own voice, may be;
and never modifying his glib whistle,
he's lone, outlined, in the leafless

oak tree. Awry as a bud
in the silver air. What are we to do?
The singular voice in the wind
falling on dead ears. Oh,

we cannot look openly
into each other's eyes.  Neither dominant,
we look at a neutral place a few inches by
our faces, rock on our feet, breathe slant.

The bird warbles and warbles.

# LIAR'S DICE

Used to mark a corner, a claim,
these totem rocks are painted into faces,
men.  I have this stamp of land
with creeping jenny, jack-in-the-pulpit,
fir trees and deep grass
I would not sell in a famine.

One way of ownership
is not to tell how much you have.
Liar's dice, the number of birds' bones
and thighs of foxes that click
on the table of the field I hold.
The checkered wind.

                The gamble to sleep
with him when someone walking
with the cool moon or in broad day
may walk into our outdoor room
and fall on us like police.

Stood like a grizzly, emblem mask
to warn away intruders, the pole reminds.
I hide and shape my place,
own each pebble, use it all.
The beautiful fish, the warm birds.
Even if shown, love, they don't know.

## WELL

At the base of the mountains,
under reddened skies, there is a clapboard house
and a pump like a muscular neck.

I was there once
between the night star and Jones' Drug Store
when I could just read signs.

I rested
on the backseat of the Bel-Air station wagon,
counting the landmarks

to keep me back
in the range songs my Aunt Pril taught me
and the feeling of cool

silver threads
my family fed me from the cowboy pump.
The water network under the desert.

# MOTHER AND DAUGHTER

Your mother's love
for potatoes, chocolate
and all things raw;
her clear beauty, and her wrath,
which changed her into statuary
and you into a scrabbling heathen,
except her blood would kneel
to no one, and she would pout
a rabbit, relenting,
is inside you like lining.
Though she die and you shred
all your clothes in a wilderness,
you'll not go naked
or feel naked hurt.
You'll not lie down alone
with a man, but love him
with the fiber and ease of the mother
and daughter, which is yourself
at thirty: fruitfuller,
letting others live in you,
lining with a thick gruel
of love their ribs.

## LET BE

"You'll split the earth in half,"
my son tells me as I spade a plot
for lady slippers and cosmos.
I pull at the burdock
root that winds like veins. "See,
those trees over there will fall." The ground makes
sense to my son. Spring is a soft, particular tangle.
We look at the leaning trees,
which have dimensions of green
only a child wants. He doesn't pick out the nest
I describe. He senses a trillion
minutes in the leaves
without counting. He sings
"four and twenty blackbirds" and
"when the pie was opened the birds
began to sing." The blood in his heart
is certain as pitch
how to heal. He hands me a wish flower.
He has ten crescent moons under his nails.

# BIRTHDAY

I screamed, we both screamed;
out of our heads, bloody and splendid.
I asked your sex

and desired only to sleep.
A nurse I will never forget
put ice on my clay thighs

and rocked me in a warm lake.
Teeth of lilies, Loreli,
I dreamt of you whole

and dear-achieved.
Sun roused us both.
Machinery of the town started up.

They brought you in,
and we began the first day.

## ADULTERY

Waking into the wind
at night, there is no child
with his voice a cracked heirloom
in his small room.
Something is broken and cold
in the swaying house.  I hear noise
like a raw-hide knot loosed
at my back.  Who let it fly?

From the patio deck I see your head
coaxed to sleep.  You have risked
breaking your nerves, stretched
on the bridge from your house to mine.
We have sailed away together
when the signs in the air were right.
In a storm the salt raises welts.
Is it you crying?

Another night.  Again we will mock them
with breakfast together.
The house wallows in calm,
but the sun will move the wind
hoarse, and we will hear it.

## WATER SOUNDS

When I walk I make a sound with my legs
like scrubbing cloth, and the scent is changed.
There is less perfume, less work to be dolled.
It is a humming, click or clean under sound
to attract: It's more fish than bird. The whine
of the dolphin. I can move as I like,
but tap my heel in a rhythm or arhythm,
and wear no ruff. Sleek or lumpy.
Basic. You can hear my sign if you like
and go walking by unperturbed. You won't.
You'll look back, think "water?" These water
                              sounds;
the wash, the rain can do without clothes
or suggestion. Water is more than sun.
I am plain. So are you. We have our hands.

64

## REPLY TO AN UNCOY LOVER

If a fly were a kiss,
I would follow you to Nigeria

and we'd lie in a corral
of grass huts, under your cloak

with dust like fur between us.
We would kiss to forget

the honeyless swarm on our heads
not unlike a bull and cow in heat,

the cow tethered, the flies passionate
but without imagination, our tails missing.

Or you could be my whale
and bring a friend to swim on the other side

as a pleasant diversion.  For a lover who thinks
he has loved top to bottom, in water and heat,

is not only a slouching beast or a cartoon flea
in a jungle of dog's hair, his nose stubbed,

he is Chanticleer, and Lancelot
with his lightening spear; king of a minute.

I hear loneliness in the wind
and you believe it is heavy breathing.

## APOGEE

In my thoughts I lean over water
letting a boat tip in such a manner
that you on shore miles away
will somehow know my body
arches as if I skim the back of my head
along the waves, as if you feel hard
in me.

          In the tide and century
of this dream I am sea mare.
You can put your palm on my flank.
I will not quake
or entirely yield.

In each other's arms
it's this way after a long time.
Or first.

          Last year I read your mind.

I can't do more.

## STILL SHOTS

I see parts of you.
Your face is a leather rose.
Your eyes ball up like caterpillars,
since for you my hand comes with a stick.
I'm not an urchin curious for your guts.

Yesterday, I watched your hand alive
on the chair arm, keeping time,
or twitching like a dreaming dog.
When pressed, your hand snapped shut.
You're not a pet for my house, I know.

I would take your heart.
I would see it as a better picture
in my hands.  I could leave no smudging.
And if I dropped it in my lap,
I never would wash the blood away.

Your legs are March and June.
Your back is a lake.
Your wishes are molten lava.
Your lips are the rim of a volcano.
I would bundle everything in my bed.

## AS YOU MIGHT CLAIM LOVE

If by blinking your eyes turn sharp
as they are bright, you see like a knife
can smell blood. Glitter: keeping watch
at the border, your fences are electric eels.
In the slightest wave of a hand from the woods
you hear a call to arms, feel the dog in you growl,
fearing the disappearance of the hand
in the strange, black woods.
Your voice a spotlight, you encircle
the small gesture, "Who goes there?" This way
                                     it grows
from nothing to a trophy or a password.
Anyway, your own, as you might claim love.

In boot camp you learned nothing subtle
about time. Your heart under house arrest,
the flick of a wrist can turn the sun black
or raise the day to the ceiling,
the way he lifts your son.
In your breast pocket is a manual
describing what you stand to lose,
whereas the dream is the uniform of the day.
As sentry you are so quickened.

## DESIRING

Winter moon.  Snow on a wizard hill
where she dreams to step from dark to dark
without shoes.  Naked,
when she could be naked in the bed
where someone lies naked as if in snow
with snow in his mouth and a snow sky overhead.

Live as a deer
when she hears a deer, moist under his seamless skin,
cough from a pure hollow.  He's on her
and all she sees is herself
and pain in his eyes, as moonlight reflects there
                            like headlights
and she breaks.

When she falls backwards, she falls into a hammock
                            of snow.
Overhead are the orbs
which her lover sees with his eyes closed.
When she falls forward, the snow kills her.
Never is her face the same for its ability
to soften, cry out, see winter.

## HISTORY OF LOVE

You stand by the mirror.
Something in the lit curve of your hip,
you daring yourself
to stagger the old light,
tells you propose a lover.

Later, when he fails to hold you,
except you see in his gentle eyes
a wanting look
and cannot tell what brightness you'd once been,
you dismiss him

and miss him with the look of absinthe,
your rumpled skirt wide as a fan,
elbows on your sad knees,
your hands between your knees,
hands large as flamingos.

## WORDS FOR GOODBYE

It will snow in May.  Boughs
will break by your leave.
The sun grown cool as night grass.

There are mornings when the apple bud, or to live
in garden air, is too forever sweet.
Over, the steady pulse of love.

Love.  The apparatus and light
of blossoms.  Petal, horn, wet weather.
Salamanders in the well.  Too sweet.

Rather have bare lightning in winter;
ignorance.  Let the new snow melt over
the tree and into the well.  Let it be clear

and odorless and cold.

# FIRST THINGS

"Watch our bees make honey in glass cases."
Billboard, Highway 70, Kansas

Drawn to and held off by another city
where I don't know the culverts and hiding
places, the open road; if I catch someone
opening Kafka's *Metamorphosis* at a light
to the identical page, I am no longer apart,
a distinctive dark beast.

Leaving
the white bed in my house to the doorway
of a similar bed in a hotel, the loins roll,
grown a little in some small direction.
I and my brother.
How many of us from the baby boom?

We have the same gross hands
or thin wrists.  Thousands of us eat
the same bite of roquefort salad.
I saw the sign to watch the bees
while traveling back in the black wind
of so many paved miles and cold faces
in their cars.

No more strange breath around my neck,
a strand of pop beads.  I settle
on first things; falling steps to the house,
the heavy sun of your word, the heart
beating differently on mine, those wings
behind your eyes, quickening home.

# IN COMMON PLACES

Wish I had been alone; your tread was a heavy cord
around my knees.  Though we had come in a friendly
way,
the need to tremble like a lake to feel the geese flock
rise,
and stopped by your form, was changing me to sump.

I breathed the air from my neck and held still,
your arm a wall around me.  Me over my head
to say the birds were strangely beautiful.
It's not that you haven't seen a miracle,

the heart of the world.  I cannot look at you,
but as we trek and haul ourselves up this hill
you may be shivering inside, your eyes on fire.
A lover swooning with your rare voice tied.

We hold and take our secrets like a sad man
with his mistress.  In common places.  A country lake,
the moon an animal torch, a cheap, gray hotel room.
But when we quiver, we quiver deep and harder.

Carol Frost was born in 1948 in Massachusetts and educated at the Sorbonne, State University of New York at Oneonta, and Syracuse University. She lives on a farm in upstate New York with her husband and their two sons, Daniel and Joel.